Ugh! Yuck! and Whoa!

What a Jerk!

WORLD BOOK

World Book, Inc.
180 North LaSalle Street
Suite 900
Chicago, Illinois 60601
USA

For information about other World Book publications, visit our website at **www.worldbook.com** or call **1-800-WORLDBK (967-5325)**.

Library of Congress Cataloging-in-Publication data has been applied for.
Title: Ugh! Yuck! and Whoa! What a Jerk!
ISBN: 978-0-7166-3712-7

Ugh! Yuck! and Whoa!
ISBN: 978-0-7166-3708-0 (set, hc)

Also available as:
ISBN: 978-0-7166-3720-2 (e-book)

1st printing July 2018

STAFF

Executive Committee

President
Jim O'Rourke

Vice President and Editor in Chief
Paul A. Kobasa

Vice President, Finance
Donald D. Keller

Vice President, Marketing
Jean Lin

Vice President, International
Maksim Rutenberg

Vice President, Technology
Jason Dole

Director, Human Resources
Bev Ecker

Editorial

Director, Print Publishing
Tom Evans

Writer
Grace Guibert

Editor
Will Adams

Manager, Contracts & Compliance (Rights & Permissions)
Loranne K. Shields

Manager, Indexing Services
David Pofelski

Librarian
S. Thomas Richardson

Digital

Director, Digital Product Development
Erika Meller

Digital Product Manager
Jonathan Wills

Manufacturing/ Production

Manufacturing Manager
Anne Fritzinger

Proofreader
Nathalie Strassheim

Graphics and Design

Senior Art Director
Tom Evans

Senior Designer
Don Di Sante

Media Editor
Rosalia Bledsoe

Special thanks to:

Nature Picture Library

Introduction

Nature is filled with some amazing creatures. From ocean bottoms to mountain tops, from hot deserts to freezing tundra, the *Ugh! Yuck! and Whoa!* books highlight the most extreme animals: the grossest, the deadliest, the strangest, and the ugliest! This book is all about animals that are rude. Some animals are rude to each other, and some animals are rude to humans! These "bad" behaviors often help animals survive in their **habitat. Habitats** are the places where animals live and grow. Animals might be rude to protect themselves from harm. Others might be mean in order to get food or water to live. Others still might just have nasty personalities! Read on to learn about the biggest jerks in the animal kingdom and why they act the way they do. This How Rude! meter will show just how big of a jerk each animal can be.

PARASITOID WASP

Whoa!

Unlike some other wasps, parasitoid wasps don't sting. So, at least they are not rude in that way!

A **parasite** is a living thing that feeds off of another living thing. Parasitoid *(PAR uh SY toyd)* wasps lay eggs on caterpillars. The eggs hatch, the baby wasps eat the insides of the caterpillar's body, and the caterpillar dies.

HOW RUDE!
HIGH

ANGLERFISH

Male anglerfish are much smaller than females. When a male anglerfish finds a female, he bites into her! He becomes fused (attached) to her body by his mouth. The male anglerfish feeds off of the female's blood for the rest of his life.

HOW RUDE!
MEDIUM

Parasite Bites

These common bugs are **parasites. Parasites** feed off of other living things. Here are some **parasites** that drink human blood! In addition to giving us itchy or painful bites, these **parasites** sometimes spread dangerous diseases.

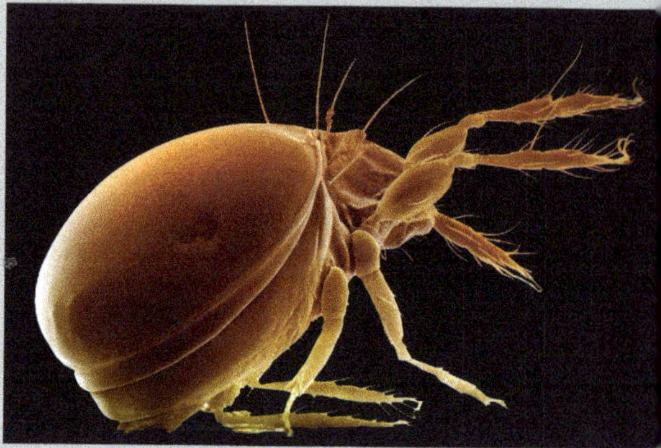

Mite

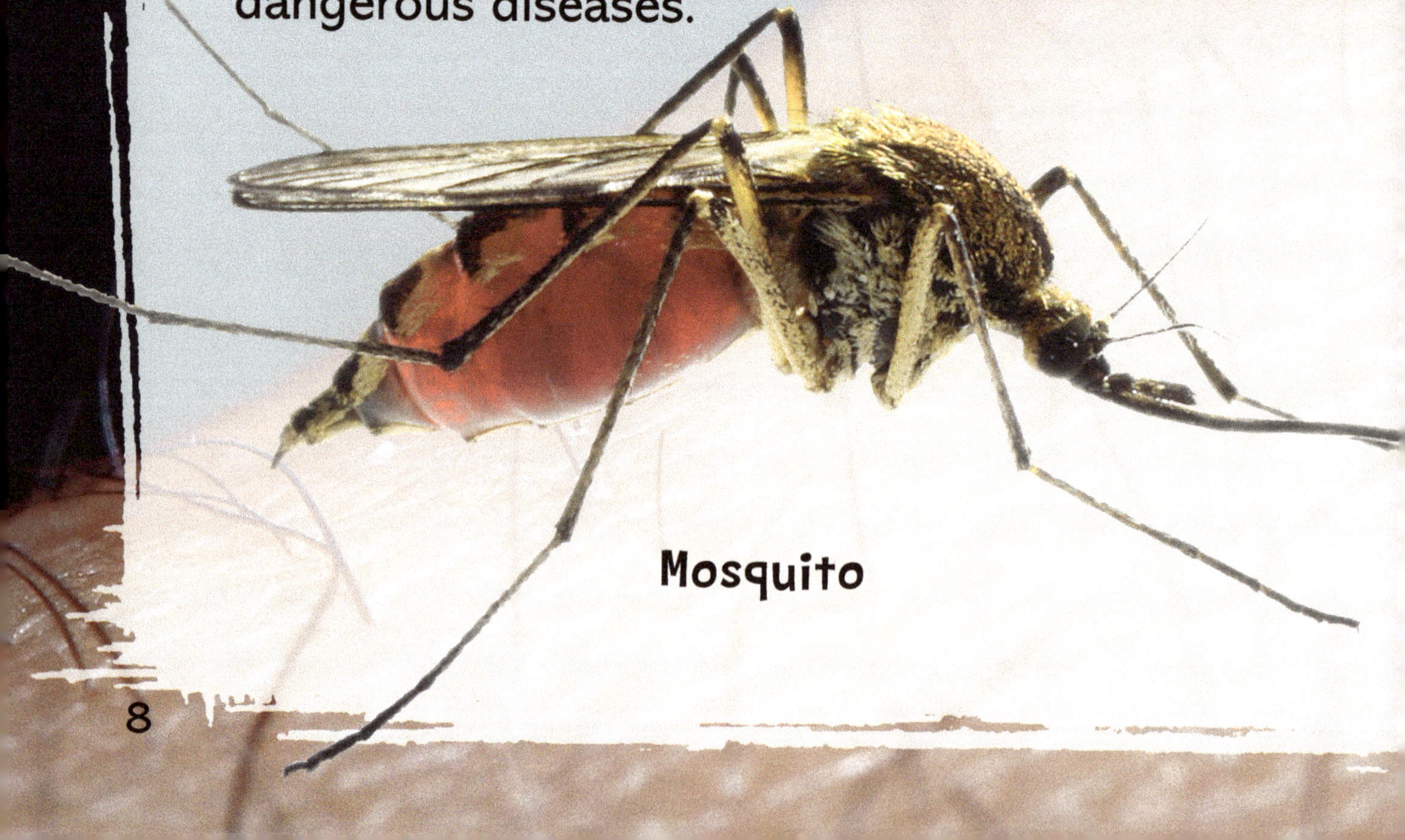

Mosquito

Louse

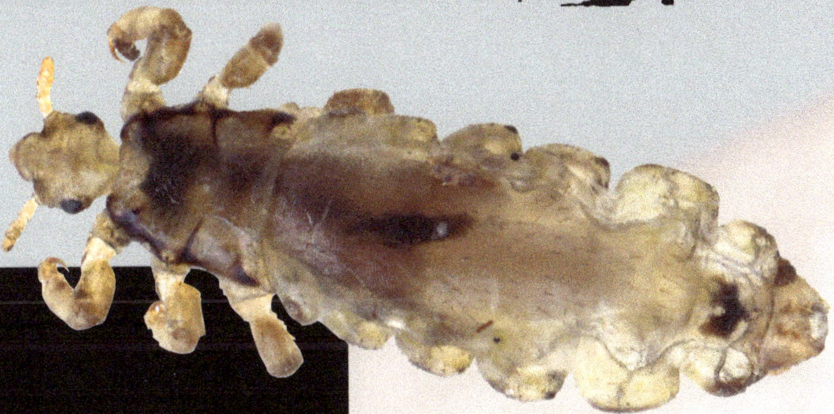

Flea

Bed bug

Tick

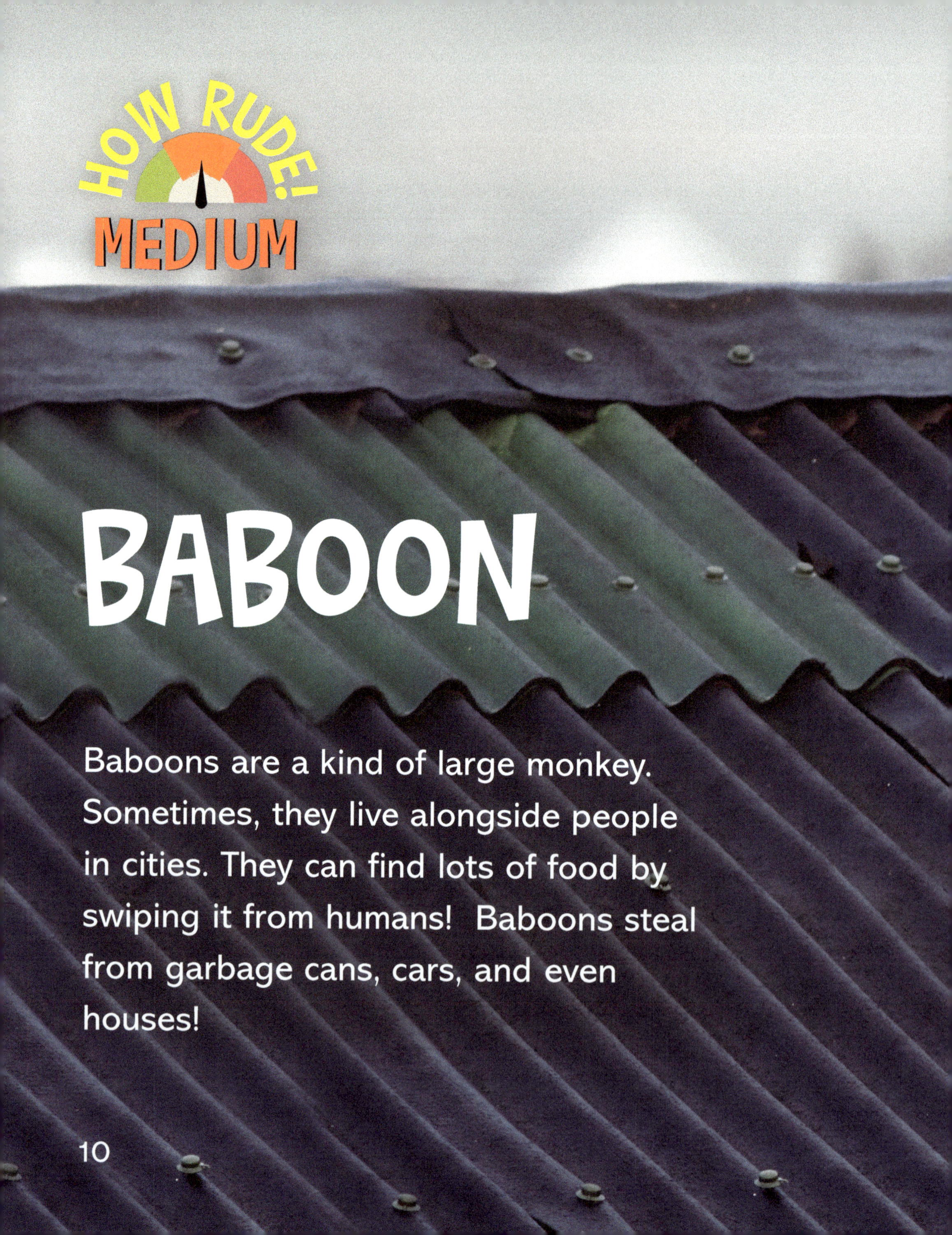

HOW RUDE!

MEDIUM

BABOON

Baboons are a kind of large monkey. Sometimes, they live alongside people in cities. They can find lots of food by swiping it from humans! Baboons steal from garbage cans, cars, and even houses!

KEA

Ugh!

Keas are **omnivores**. This means they eat plants and animals. Keas will eat just about anything: bugs, fruits, dead animals, and even other birds! They are the only kind of parrot that eats meat. A few even perch on live sheep and peck at them for meat!

This funny parrot is fearless around humans. The kea often flies right up to people, their cars, and their houses to peck around for food. Keas can be total jerks. They might pull off pieces of cars with their beaks!

HOW RUDE!
MEDIUM

HOW RUDE!
MEDIUM

CHIMPANZEE

When chimpanzees get angry, they often throw rocks or sticks. When chimpanzees are taken from their natural **habitat** and kept in places like zoos, they might get angry more often. If they can't get their hands on rocks, they sometimes throw their own poo!

CUCKOO

The common cuckoo, a type of bird, does not care for its own babies. Instead, the cuckoo lays its eggs in another bird's nest! The cuckoo parent leaves its eggs to be hatched and raised by the other bird. After the cuckoo chick hatches, it pushes all the other eggs or chicks out of the nest. This cuckoo chick is being fed by a type of bird called a reed warbler.

HOW RUDE!
HIGH

EMPEROR PENGUIN

It's hard to raise a baby in Antarctica. Not all penguin babies survive the cold winter. If a mother emperor penguin loses her baby, she might kidnap another! Sometimes, lots of mothers even fight with each other over a baby to steal.

HOW RUDE!
HIGH

FALSE CLEANER BLENNY

This little fish looks just like another one, called the bluestreak cleaner wrasse *(ras)*. The bluestreak cleaner wrasse cleans **parasites** off of larger fish in the ocean.

These bigger fish allow wrasses to swim through their mouths and gills to pick off **parasites.** The false cleaner blenny pretends to be the bluestreak cleaner wrasse. When it gets close to bigger fish, it takes a bite out of the fish instead!

Whoa!

Big fish, like the one pictured here, let bluestreak cleaner wrasses swim right into their mouths!

HONEY BADGER

The honey badger is a small mammal that looks like a skunk. This little creature loves to pick fights—even with animals that are much bigger than it! The honey badger can put up a tough fight. It might take on lions, hyenas, zebras, and snakes!

HOW RUDE!

LOW

Whoa!

Honey badgers can take on just about any snake. Honey badgers are immune to (not harmed by) snakes' **venom**!

TONGUE-EATING LOUSE

This little **parasite** swims into a fish through its gills. It attaches to the fish's tongue and sucks blood from it. Over time, the tongue shrivels up and falls out! The tongue-eating louse then acts as the fish's new tongue.

HOW RUDE!
HIGH

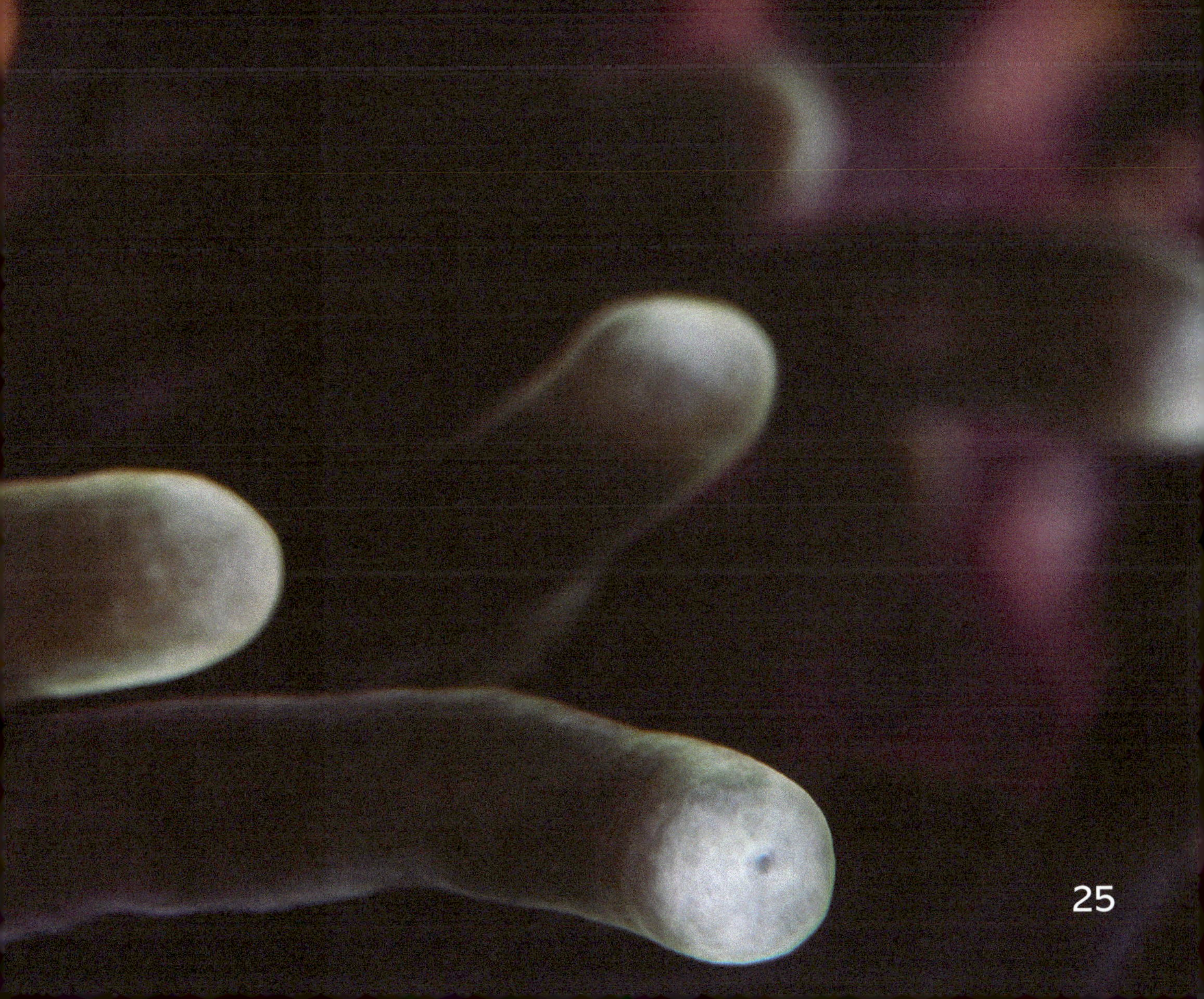

TASMANIAN DEVIL

Tasmanian devils get their name from their scary, bad behavior. When they feel threatened, Tasmanian devils open their mouths wide to show their sharp teeth while they screech and snarl.

HOW RUDE! LOW

Whoa!

You might recognize this animal from television. The Tasmanian Devil, sometimes called Taz, is one of the Looney Tunes™ characters!

COOKIECUTTER SHARK

This small shark has a long, powerful body and razor-sharp teeth. Its circular mouth makes round holes like a cookie cutter! It races up to a large ocean animal, takes a huge bite, and swims away before the victim can react.

HOW RUDE! MEDIUM

Some large ocean animals, such as whales and dolphins, survive many attacks from cookiecutter sharks.

STOAT

Stoats, sometimes called ermines *(UR muhns)*, are weasels with white coats of fur. They normally eat small rodents and rabbits. But they will steal food if it's available!

HOW RUDE!
LOW

Whoa!

This stoat is trying to steal fish that are hanging on a fishing line.

SLAVE-MAKING ANT

HOW RUDE!
HIGH

Slave-making ants invade the nests of other ants, kidnap young ants, and bring them back to their own colony! These young ants grow up as members of the slave-making colony. They help to build the nest, care for the young, and hunt for food.

HERRING GULL

HOW RUDE!

LOW

The herring gull, which you might know as the seagull, is a funny bird. It eats almost anything—including scraps of garbage! They might take food from garbage cans, streets, or right out of your hand!

RACCOON

The raccoon has a patch of black fur around its eyes. It looks like the mask a thief might wear! And raccoons live up to that appearance. They are **nocturnal**, which means they sleep during the day and move about at night. They steal eggs from birds' nests and human food from garbage cans.

HOW RUDE!
HIGH

Animal Thieves

Octopus

Octopuses are strong and smart. They have been known to steal crabs and fish out of fishing boats!

Arctic fox

An Arctic fox's white fur helps it blend into the snow. Its camouflage allows arctic foxes to sneak right up to birds' nests to steal eggs.

Squirrel

When squirrels get hungry, they'll snag any food they can! A squirrel might take vegetables, flowers, and fruits from gardens, or it might take nuts and seeds from people's homes. Squirrels even steal food from other squirrels.

Hyena

Hyenas travel in big groups. If they come upon another animal, like a lion, that has found food, hyenas work together to drive that animal away! Then they steal the food.

PRAYING MANTIS

Praying mantises are hunting insects. Sometimes, a female praying mantis will eat her mate. The male praying mantis can continue to move for a while even after his head has been eaten!

HOW RUDE!
HIGH

HYENA

There is serious sibling rivalry among young hyenas. Not long after they are born, hyena cubs will attack each other! About one in every four hyena cubs dies in these fights.

HOW RUDE!
HIGH

CAMEL

Don't get too close to a camel. When camels get annoyed, they spit on whatever—or whoever—is bugging them! And it isn't just spit that they spray. They also throw up whatever is in their stomach. Yuck!

HOW RUDE! HIGH

Whoa!

Camels are known for the humps on their back. Some people believe that the humps hold water. Instead they hold fat that the camels can use for energy when food and water are hard to find. If camels use up all the fat, their humps can get saggy!

Glossary

Habitat

the place where a plant or animal naturally lives and grows.

Nocturnal

active at night.

Omnivore

an animal that eats plants and animals.

Parasite

a living thing that attaches itself to another living thing for food and survival.

Thief

someone who steals, especially one who steals secretly and without using force.

Venom

a liquid that an animal makes to stun, injure, or kill another animal through biting or stinging.

Index

Acknowledgments

Cover: © ullstein bild/Getty Images; © Anup Shah, Nature Picture Library

4-5 © Elizabeth O. Weller, Shutterstock; © James Dunbar, Nature Picture Library

6-7 © Solvin Zankl, Nature Picture Library

8-9 © Kim Taylor, Nature Picture Library; © Visuals Unlimited/ Nature Picture Library; © John Abbott, Nature Picture Library; © Stephen Dalton, Nature Picture Library; © Doug Wechsler, Nature Picture Library

10-11 © Cyril Ruoso, Nature Picture Library

12-13 © Brent Stephenson, Nature Picture Library

14-15 © Anup Shah, Nature Picture Library

16-17 © David Tipling, 2020VISION/Nature Picture Library

18-19 © Bill Coster, Alamy Images

20-21 © Reinhard Dirscherl, Getty Images; © Pascal Kobehn, Nature Picture Library

22-23 © Vincent Grafhorst, Minden Pictures; © Petlin Dmitry,Shutterstock

24-25 © Vincent Truchet, Alamy Images

26-27 © John Cancalosi, Nature Picture Library; © Looney Tunes/ Warner Bros. Entertainment Inc.

28-29 © Bill Curtsinger, National Geographic Creative; © David Fleetham, Nature Picture Library

30-31 © Erlend Haarberg, Nature Picture Library

32-33 © Kim Taylor, Nature Picture Library

34-35 © Sam Hobson, Nature Picture Library

36-37 © Michael Durham, Nature Picture Library

38-39 © Sergey Gorshkov, Nature Picture Library; © Yellow Cat/ Shutterstock; © Mike Read, Nature Picture Library; © Denis-Huot, Nature PIcture Library

40-41 © Jose B. Ruiz, Nature PIcture Library

42-43 © Denis-Huot, Getty Images

44-45 © ullstein bild/Getty Images

www.ingramcontent.com/pod-product-compliance
Ingram Content Group UK Ltd.
Pitfield, Milton Keynes, MK11 3LW, UK
UKHW061957290726
14090UKWH00021B/1257

9 780716 650850